Revlon Dolls

Joan Hancock–Dow

Table of Contents

On the Cover

Clockwise from top left:
18 inch Revlon doll in taffeta & lace & organza gown
15 inch Revlon doll in "Cherries a la Mode" nylon dress
10 1/2 in Little Miss Revlon doll in "Princess" outfit
22 inch Revlon doll in "Kissing Pink" striped cotton outfit
25 inch Revlon doll in tiered lace "Glamour Gown"
20 inch Revlon doll in "Snow Peach Bride" outfit

Copyright 2018 by Joan Hancock-Dow

Dedication

This book is dedicated to my mother, Ruth Tomlinson & her father Martin Englund who facilitated my acquiring my first Revlon doll.

Acknowledgements

Kathy Barna: Revlon Dolls and their Look-Alikes
Robert Tonner
Dr. Katherine Beier
Colleen Thompson
Judith Izen: Collector's Guide to Ideal Dolls, editions 1, 2 & 3
to order: http://www.dollsofourchildhood.com/
Theriault's
Barb Walker: http://www.angelfire.com/ultra/revlondoll/index.html
Chris Carrick
Pat Derelanko
Gail Gavit
Florence Roberts
Sandy Herman
Deanna Tomlinson Miller
Sherry Kriesel

My History & the
Evolution of this project

I was born in 1946, the first year of the baby boomers, & raised in Minneapolis. I have spent most of my life in that area but have also lived in Eau Claire, WI & Los Angeles. I was a psychiatric RN for 35 years. I got my 18 inch Revlon in 1957. My mother & I sewed for her throughout my life. I didn't become a collector of Revlon dolls or a researcher until the early 1990s when events converged to prompt an interest in antiques. I started collecting Barbies after finding an original RN uniform complete with accessories. I discovered that 2 nurse colleagues were also doll collectors. We shared a love of Barbies for several years.

Around this time I also thought it would be fun to have a trunk set of reproduction outfits for my Revlon doll in "all" the original styles, not knowing how many there actually were. I wound up with a lovely collection then the sewer I'd been using quit & didn't save her patterns. I realized that I needed to make my own patterns, not only for myself but for the many nude or poorly dressed Revlon dolls I saw for sale on Ebay. I had already been making repro Barbie patio hats for about 10 years & selling them on ebay. I started researching Revlon dolls by networking with collectors & dealers. It was frustrating that there was so much mis-information about what outfits & dolls were genuine Ideal-made. Many genuine outfits were never tagged. Since there were already a few doll informational websites, I thought I'd share what I'd learned with one of them. I offered. Nothing happened. So I realized that in order to get the information out there, I had to do my own website. I bought a software package & dug in. I retired from nursing in 2003 & soon after got my website up & running. Right about the same time, Kathy Barna published her book "Revlon dolls & their lookalikes". She put me in touch with other people doing research on Revlon dolls & the adventure picked up speed. Eventually collectors started to offer photos of dolls & outfits that I didn't have on my website so I no longer felt I had to own everything pictured. Over the years I've made a point of meeting most of my contributors in person.

Around 2006 I applied to the United Federation of Doll Clubs for a research scholarship. I was turned down because the only stipends available at that time were for antique or composition dolls. I wrote a letter to them pointing out that if they wanted to attract younger members, especially baby boomers, they should really look at being more accepting/encouraging of collectors of dolls from that era. My letter had an impact. They spoke to one of their benefactors (Becky Wallace) who donated the money to start a scholarship fund for "modern dolls". The next year (2007) I applied again & won the first of these scholarships.

New information continues to surface, although rarely, so I decided it was time to put all this information down in hard copy form. Over the last 15 years or so, with the help of other collectors, we have attempted to fit the pieces into the puzzle (ie was it made by Ideal? is it tagged? was it sold by just one vendor as a special sale? does it have a style #? did it come on a doll with a unique body? was it produced early or late during Ideal's production period? how rare is it?

Revlon Dolls

Revlon dolls were sold by Ideal Toy Corporation from late 1956 thru 1960. It was a unique time in history, with a large increase in post WWII pre-teens (baby boomers), a strong interest in fashion by females of all ages, a prosperous economy, the invention of vinyl & man-made products for doll hair, & an increase in acceptance of "full figured" dolls. Charles Revson initially didn't want to sponsor a doll but later agreed when he realized how many pre-teen doll owners would soon be using lipstick & makeup.

Sizes – Revlon first released 3 sizes – 18", 20" & 22". Then came the 10 ½" Little Miss Revlon doll in '57, the 15" doll ('58 & '59), & for a very brief time in '58, the 25" doll. Each size has its own unique appearance apart from its size, & the 18" doll even had 4 different face molds. There are also <u>late production</u> Revlon dolls that are shorter than indicated by their markings (ie VT18 dolls are 17" & VT20 are 19"). These dolls also sometimes have a different head & face appearance, sometimes called a "pixie face.

***From this point on, I will often use the terms "larger dolls" to refer to all sizes of Revlon dolls larger than Little Miss Revlon.

Little Miss Revlons will sometimes be referred to as "little dolls" or LMRs. Larger dolls are also known as Miss Revlons.

Markings – Most are marked on the neck – "IDEAL DOLL" then "VT" followed by the doll's height (10 1/2, 18, 20, 22, 25). There are also markings of just the height number inside each arm & leg. 15" dolls are marked on the upper back "IDEAL 15N".

Bodies – All dolls have head, shoulder (arm), leg & waist joints. A few dolls have knee joints. Limbs are attached to torsos with flange molded ends as are waist joints on larger dolls. Little dolls are strung with one band from head through upper torso to hips. Some of the larger dolls' heads are attached with wood blocks & metal bolts running from head through to hips. (see photo on page 65) The larger dolls' joints have held up extreme-ly well over time whereas almost all of the little dolls have need-ed or are needing to be restrung. Limbs are vinyl, some harder than others, & some are painted. Occasionally the upper torso of an LMR is painted. A very few dolls (18" & 20") have a walking mechanism with or without bendable knees (20" only). Rare-ly, some larger dolls have bendable elbows but I have come to believe these were probably not made by Ideal (ie. not genuine Revlon). One leg is usually a tad longer than the other. Many believe this is so they can be posed as if they are walking but recent findings indicate it just might have been a factor in the manufacturing process. There were some dolls manufactured with Revlon markings that had bendable elbows. I think most collectors & researchers now believe these were dolls sold by other companies that may have purchased some parts from Ideal.

Heads – All dolls have vinyl heads with rooted, high quality saran hair that withstands washing & resetting quite well. All dolls have sleep eyes – most are blue but other colors are also often found. LMR's eyelashes are molded + painted. Larger dolls' eyelashes are brush + painted. Ears are usually pierced. Hair color was generally blond, light brown or auburn, with occasional brunettes & ash blondes – these colors have often lost their intensity over time. All dolls have bangs & hair length is usually shoulder length or longer. Very rarely, larger dolls have been found with short pixie hair styles, side part & widow's peak hair styles. Larger dolls original hair styles usually have hair on either side of the face pulled up to the crown & secured with a rubber band (standard for Queen of Diamonds dolls) & the rest falling in soft curls behind the ears; or pulled back behind the ears & secured with u-shaped pins. A few had upswept hair styles. 5th Avenue dolls often have right side low ponytails. Little & 15" dolls had gold elastic head bands pulling the hair back from the face. LMR's have either high short pony tails rolled into a bun, or short bobs, with a few having longer hair.

Makeup – All dolls had red painted lips, fingernails & toenails. Some dolls have added cheek color (also known as "high color").

Price – American Character's Sweet Sue Sophisticate, & Madame Alexander's Cissy came out about the same time but Revlon sold a high quality doll that was cheaper, so they were a huge hit immediately. Larger dolls sold for between $12.98 & $22.99, depending on doll size & expense of the outfit. Interest-

ingly, the bendable knee doll was the least expensive of the larger dolls, probably because the pants outfit was considered to
be worth less. Little dolls sold for $2.98 in the basic underwear
outfit, or up to $8 dressed. There were also LMR gift sets, which
included a doll & 4 outfits. Toward the end of production in '59,
there were cheaper 17" & 19" dolls released, that still had the VT
18 & 20 markings but were made with lower quality vinyl & had
cheaper outfits & accessories. Many did not have earring holes.
Some of this cheaper vinyl has now turned an orangey color.

Revlon doll Outfits

As with most fashion dolls, Revlon dolls are mostly about
the clothes.

The Little Miss Revlon dolls were often sold in just bra, girdle,
shoes, nylons, drop pearl earrings & hairnet, with outfits sold
separately. But they were also sold dressed.

There were very few extra outfits sold for the larger dolls (mostly 18"), whereas there were hundreds sold for the 10 ½" size (ap-
proximately 100 known numbers with many variations, many con-
firmed Ideal outfits with unknown style numbers & about 15 known
numbers to unknown styles). The reason this list is still in question,
in spite of many researchers toiling on this project for years, is because Ideal's records of what they produced were lost when they
were sold to CBS toys in 1983 & then that company went out of
business shortly after. Many outfits were never tagged.

Many of the dresses for all sizes have a drop waist, which was a
popular style at the time.

The 15" dolls had fewer outfits, no hats, no stoles, no rhinestone
jewelry, & different shoes than the crisscross elastic ones of the
other larger dolls.

The 25" doll had glamour gowns in 2 styles; 22" dolls had glamour gowns in 10 styles

Labels

- On larger dolls: large streamers reading "Revlon Doll" on the outside coming from the waist seam – often torn off by original owners; occasionally tagged with small labels inside

- On little dolls: small labels reading "Ideal" inside the garments, but some original outfits were never factory labeled. A few have outside labels like the larger dolls

*Only about ½ of garments of all sizes were marked which is what has made research to determine what is original so difficult.

Accessories

- Little dolls had panty girdle, bra, drop pearl earrings, plastic open toe heels, nylons with back seams, & hairnet. Very few LMR original outfits included a pearl necklace. LMR earrings often had hooked wires to keep them securely in the doll, so beware of potential damage to the ears if pulled out. Some of the outfits included purses, hats, belts, petticoats, panties, scarves, & flowers.

- Larger dolls usually had pink taffeta panties & petticoats, nylons with back seams, pearl necklaces (open chokers or longer/graduated with box clasps) & pearl drop earrings (1 or 2 round pearls, or teardrop). All except `15" size Cherries A La Mode dolls came with straw cloche style hats. Most Queen of Diamonds & Glamour dolls had rhinestone necklaces, rhinestone drop earrings (teardrop or round) a rhinestone ring on the left hand & some had rabbit fur stoles. Snow Peach bride had teardrop pearl earrings, necklace & rhinestone ring.

Shoes

- 18"-25" dolls almost always had black plastic heels with crisscross black elastic, except bride dolls that had white – this style is NEVER original for the 15" & 10 ½" *Glamour outfits often had gold crisscross shoes.

- 10 ½" were open toe plastic – white, black, aqua, or red.

- 15" were the most varied & hard to determine if they're original – black or white plastic with straight-across elastic strips; or all plastic similar to the LMR shoes in white or black.

Outfits for the larger Revlon Dolls

(15 inch, 18 inch, 20 inch, 22 inch & 25")

Some of the more well-known that were often named for Revlon lipstick colors

"Kissing Pink"

- Striped cotton dresses – pink, blue, yellow, lilac ¼" stripe; bright yellow, aqua, red; tan or salmon in 3/8" stripe.

- Taffeta square neck dresses – salmon/pink, aqua, yellow, or blue.

- Cotton print boat neck dresses w/ circle skirts & solid color nylon organza neck + trim.

- Linen dresses w/ black lines running through fabric, bow & flower @ waist – brick red, rose, yellow, lilac or gold.

- Heart dresses – pink or navy nylon; red, navy, or pink taffeta.

- Jacket dresses – woven cotton print dresses with removable cotton knit short bolero jacket; some jackets have woven collar matching dress print – various versions in combinations of red, yellow or blue.

"Cherries A La Mode"

- Nylon print dresses – pink floral; pink, navy, light blue, or yellow cherries print.

- Pink or blue taffeta dress w/ white eyelet overdress.

- Solid color sleeveless taffeta dress in pink or aqua.

- Pink square neck dress w/ green flocked swirls (this came w/ a clear hatbox).

- Navy nylon floral w/ square neck.

- Taffeta dress with low cowl front & lace insert + hat – navy, green or pink – 18" & 20" size – sometimes sold on dolls with side part hair styles.

- Red on white dotted Swiss dresses w/ red trim.

"Queen of Diamonds"

- Velveteen dresses + rabbit fur stole – red, kelly green, teal, or blue.

- Brocade dresses + rabbit fur stole – gold, pink, blue, green, red, or aqua.

- Red velveteen top with white satin skirt (or white nylon gauze skirt) dresses + rabbit stole.

- Gold lame bodice w/ cotton skirt dresses, w/ or w/o red or black velveteen coat + long gold scarf.

- Tiered lace dresses + rabbit stole – pink or blue.

- Chintz dresses w/ low neckline, white collar & plastic floral pin @ center front neck.

"Evening Star" – gold taffeta dress + velveteen coat w/ fur trim (for walkers).

"Snow Pink" – aqua square neck sleeveless taffeta dress w/ short tulle overskirt (for walkers). Lace, taffeta & tulle gown – pale pink lace over taffeta bodice, tulle over taffeta skirt, waist sash/bow – identical to LMR #9160.

"Swirling Formal" – red or kelly green satin strapless top w/ white satin long skirt (from Montgomery Wards). Taffeta organza gown with long velvet ribbon streamers on Sears Happi-Time doll – taffeta with organza overskirt, built-in organza shawl sleeves, long velvet ribbon streamers from bodice – yellow, blue or pink.

"Deb Basic Doll Chemise" (teddy).

"Deb" gowns – various formal gowns that were sold separately for the Deb dolls.

"5th Avenue" – woven cotton pants, cotton knit body suits or onesies, & some had unlined open velour jackets – were sold on 20" bendable knee dolls.

"Snow Peach Bride" – floor length lace gown w/ long sleeves, lace overlay skirt & separate overlay ruffled panel in front, satin underskirt, sequin trim @ jewel neckline & waist, net veil w/

lace edging, oval headdress w/ arrangement of orange blossoms & lace edge.

"Delightful Organdy" – organdy dresses w/ white flocked flowers & lace + black ribbon @ waist – green, yellow, or pink prints.

"7R2" – Cotton print dress w/ solid color cowl neck, waistband and sleeve bands – light blue/pink, navy/pink, or red/gold.

Halter Sundress – black velvet halter-top dress w/ red or turquoise polished cotton skirt – also came in LMR size.

Mustard color 2 piece cotton print dress w/ black ric-rac – was sold to go with Deb doll.

Nylon Dress w/ floral embossing, white lace & black velvet ribbon trim – blue dress w/ white embossing or pink dress w/ blue embossing, low cut neckline, built-in cap sleeves, ribbon/white lace/rhinestones down center front of bodice, circle skirt, sewn-in petticoat; may have come with matching stretch girdle-only 18" size has been seen.

Paisley dress – pink or blue cotton w/ white collar – only 20" size has been seen.

Faille coat – aqua princess style with matching hat – in 20" & LMR sizes.

Square neck, taffeta or faille, short sleeve dress w/ white crochet lace trim in "V" formation from shoulders to waist – mauve, gold or dusty green – 20" size only.

"Glamour Dolls" – various evening gowns for 22" & 25" dolls.

Brown cotton leaf print dress w/ brown fabric hat sold separately for 15" dolls (in Izen's "Ideal Dolls" 2nd & 3rd edition).

Cleaning & Restoration

Cleaning

First of all, do as little as necessary – better to have a somewhat dirty doll than a doll damaged by chemicals. Same with the outfits: strong cleaning products can break down vinyl & spot removers can cause bleaching over time.

Clean the body with gentle detergent solution, or a product made for vinyl dolls – don't immerse the doll's head.

Clean the hair with gentle dish detergent, combing through gently & set with narrow rollers (such as perm rollers) & perm papers. Roll hair vertically on the doll's head. Air dry at least 24 hours, face down, in case any water got into the eye cavities.

**In my experience, dry brittle hair is wonderfully restored using Twin Pines of Maine conditioner – I use it full strength on wet hair or spray on with half strength solution. Some dolls have hair that has wonderful curl memory & just scrunching the hair after washing, then letting it air dry brings it back to like-new condition.

Eyes – A drop of fine household oil on a Q-tip can brighten & clean eyes, then place doll face down. If mildew is present, use alcohol first.

Green ear is a problem with vintage vinyl dolls & is both a bacterial & a chemical reaction process. Apply rubbing alcohol with a Q-tip, followed by Remove-zit (Twin Pines of Maine) or skin cleanser for acne (ex. oxy 10) & sun, with only the spot exposed. With Little Miss Revlon heads, remove the head & do this 2-step process both inside & out. <u>Do not try to remove the head of a larger doll</u>.

NOT ALL SPOTS CAN BE REMOVED SO, TO BE SAFE, REPLACE ALL METAL JEWELRY WITH HIGH QUALITY metal or plastic (such as pieces of bridal spray) & BEWARE OF ANCHORED EAR WIRES – CUT THEM SO THEY DON'T TEAR EARS. Green stains are also common on the necks of Queen of Diamonds dolls – the rhinestone necklaces are made from metal that is not kind to these older vinyl dolls. I recommend that they be removed but kept with the dolls.

Smelly dolls from smoke or mildew – the best remedy I know of is fresh air. Place doll in a safe shady place outside; sometimes more than a one day treatment is necessary. This may not fix the problem completely but will make an improvement. I've heard that tea tree oil heavily diluted with water is a good option to treat mold/mildew.

Twin Pines of Maine has many products for cleaning & conditioning dolls & their clothing – all of them are excellent in my experience, although *I don't personally guarantee the results of any of these products.*

http://www.twinpines.com/products

I do not recommend washing any of the taffeta, satin, brocade or velveteen clothing – dry clean if necessary. Hand wash cotton items & air dry them. Taffeta petticoats if used are almost always limp. I use several coats of spray starch, hanging them over a detergent bottle & hand smoothing after each spray. Pressing undoes the stiffening to some degree. I believe that shaking & airing to remove dust is in many cases the safest &

best way to clean valuable old doll clothing.

Repairing dolls

If flange molded joints are damaged, I know of no way to repair/ restore these parts. If you want to keep the doll & display it, the joint could be super glued together & might hold up for display purposes, but of course would no longer turn.

Little Miss Revlon dolls are strung & almost all need to be re-strung if they haven't already been done. I recommend covered cording (1/16" – 1/8") but thick rubber bands are also available for this purpose. If you don't want to attempt this yourself, there are several people offering this on ebay & other places on the internet.

The following people have offered their services to restring LMRs for a fee. They are Revlon collectors & have lovingly restored their own dolls & others of my acquaintance.

Terry Siegwald
ladybugzdollz@yahoo.com

or

Jenny Eastlick
52bkwalker@gmail.com

**Directions for restringing LMRs if you want to do this yourself:

http://www.argomo.com/lmr.htm
(this old doll hospital)

Body parts that have peeling paint, are faded or have missing paint (such as nails & lips):

Limbs that have paled: Paling legs is a common condition with bendable knee dolls. I have accommodated this where only one leg is pale by using a white nylon on the darker leg & a brown nylon on the pale leg. Since these parts aren't painted, the only other option I know of is to have the pale leg air brushed. Some collectors have replaced defective body parts by harvesting the arms or legs of donor dolls.

I've been told that a product to use to get the old paint off is Goof Off. Use it in a well ventilated area. It takes just a bit of rubbing. I have not tried this myself.

Repainting lipstick & nails – use acrylic paint & just a few hairs of a child's paintbrush with a steady hand. DO NOT USE MARK-ERS, the color spreads & you will have red spread all over the doll's face in a short time.

Replacing eyelashes & hair plugs – it can be done using hair from a donor doll but this very difficult & I have never tried it.

Replacing or switching heads on the larger dolls has been done but if the doll has an internal rod, (see page 65) it may not be possible. I had one done by a doll hospital once but they had to borrow a fire station rod cutter to do it & then replace the head without the support of the rod.

Replacing missing clothing

Original clothing for Little Miss Revlon is fairly easy to find on Ebay, Pinterest & Ruby Lane. For larger Revlon dolls, that is not the case, which is why I started making patterns so naked Revlon dolls could have fashions as close to the originals as present day fabrics allow. Upon occasion I have also found wonderful vintage fabrics at thrift shops that could be recycled into repro clothing. Several Ebay vendors sell vintage style clothing for Revlon dolls.

Hard copies of the patterns can be ordered by writing to me at jjdow@pclink.com. $5 Payment by Paypal to that same address. PDF format copies can also be emailed for you to print. $3 again by Paypal. These include:

- 5th Avenue pants outfit for 20"
- Cherries a la Mode nylon dress for 15", 18", 20" & 22"
- Kissing Pink striped dress with undies in all sizes 15", 18", 20" & 22" (all in one pattern)
- Kissing Pink boat neck dress with undies for sizes 15" & 18"
- Kissing Pink Square neck dress with undies for 18", 20" & 22"
- Little Miss Revlon accessories
- Queen of Diamonds velveteen dress with stole & undies for 18", 20" & 22"
- Tiered lace gown for 25" doll

Shoes are often missing or in need of repair. The elastic can be replaced fairly easily with a small stapler, hot glue gun, & felt. Elastic should be 1/4" wide. Do not try to replace the studs originally holding the elastic – the base of the shoe could crack. If you want to buy repro replacement shoes, the following Ebay vendors have them.

- one..more..time
- elfcrafters
- pinkink509

Many ebay vendors make repro jewelry for Revlon dolls, in some cases better quality than the originals.

Original petticoats which have lost their crispness can be partially restored by using several applications of spray starch, airdrying between each coat & not pressing (which takes out some of the stiffness) but just hand-smoothing out the wrinkles while wet.

If you are determined to find original clothing for your doll (as I have been), it will require patience & searching Ebay & Ruby Lane regularly. I have even, upon occasion, had to buy a doll in order to get the outfit.

Little Miss Revlon Outfits with style numbers if known

9000 – Little Miss Revlon Doll in box wearing bra, girdle, nylons & shoes +pearl drop earrings

9010 - Little Miss Revlon gift box
*included doll wearing bra, girdle, nylons & shoes; 4 outfits, which varied but often included a coat outfit, night wear & 2 day outfits
*sometimes non-Ideal clothing or clothing from a Crown Princess have shown up in these sets

9023 – Lounging Outfit
Long sleeved red/black/gold cotton Eastern style knee length top that crosses over, has one white snap fastener & gold braid trim; matching capri pants with gold elastic waistband

9024 – Red Knit Dress
Red & white cotton knit dress w/ stole & white daisy trim - matches coat 9427-6

9030 - Ice Skater
Red velvet long sleeve dress, fuzzy white trim at wrists & neck, red calico lining in skirt; red tights & white skates with red bias tape edged tops, metal blades; matching hat has same calico lining & fur trim *Hat photo from Colleen Thompson

9031 – Prom Formal
2 tier strapless yellow/blue dotted Swiss ankle length gown w/ lace trim, lined with sheer pale yellow and below that a sheer blue lining, cut shorter than the yellow lining,
ribbon belt, 2 snap closure in back

9033 – Nylon Party Dress
Flocked floral dress w/ elastic @ waist & neck, lace @ neck & edges of short sleeves, velvet ribbon & ruffled tulle near hem; came w/ hat, crinoline & shoes *set on right from the collection of Colleen Thompson
- has also been seen in navy blue

9034 – Taffeta Formal
Called "Charity Ball" in Wards catalog – off white taffeta skirt w/ darker bodice, hanging white/gold rickrack & flowers or large bow @ waist, crinoline; tagged - bodice colors were black, dark blue, lilac, gold, sky blue, red, green, tan & purple *gown in the middle is from Pat Derelanko *gown on right is from Colleen Thompson

9036 – Brown Coat
Brown cotton flared coat w/ one white snap @ waist, white collar & cuffs + matching hat with wire inside crown

9037- Orange Dress
Solid orange dress w/ white organdy collar, 2 white snaps on front (or back like here) & black lace trim on collar, skirt & hem; black lacy circle hat, crinoline, panties

9040 - Bridal Outfit
Lace gown w/ high neck, long sleeves, opaque raglan under-bodice, gold/white braid @ hem & neck, clear sequins @ waist, taffeta underskirt w/ picot trimmed hem, flowers over each ear, net veil, flower bouquet (from Katherine Beier)

9041 – Bridesmaid / Halter
Formal
Halter top, 2 tiers of tulle over
satin, gold braid around
neckline in front & back, satin
ribbons attached that tie
around neck; large flowers on
bodice & matching flowers on
hat
*note this hat is different than
the other bridesmaids' hats;
gathered tulle piece that may
be a stole; 2 square snaps on
back; tagged
*from Katherine Beier

9051 – Scotch Dress
Solid red cotton dress w/ plaid diagonal sash & matching
plaid tam

9052 – Cotton Plaid Dress
Red plaid dress w/ white butterfly shoulders, lace trim, 2
snaps on back + panty (a pink print version is Crown
Princess)
(from Pat Derelanko)

9053 - Striped Dress w/ V Collar
Green or purple striped short sleeve cotton dress w/ rickrack trimmed solid V collar & pocket on skirt – tagged; came w/ panties & signature purse

9054 – Halter Dress
Black velvet halter top   print cotton skirt + panty - skirt came in red/gold/black & aqua/gold/black versions

9055 - Raincoat
Vinyl hooded coat w/contrasting trim, belt, boots & tote bag came in beige w/ aqua trim, black w/ white trim, white w/ red corduroy trim, black/white stripe, red, & red/white stripe; hood has a hole in the back for ponytail & is lined with corduroy

9056 - Windmill Print Dress
White dress w/ pink or blue stripes, black windmills, black rick-rack

9060 - 3 piece Playsuit
Cotton, solid color, 1-piece halter Capri playsuit w/ tie-on yellow print skirt, white coolie hat w/ yellow bias trim - came in orange, pink & peach versions

9061- Toreador Outfit
Black velvet Capri pants w/ white sheer open front blouse & yellow, blue, red or green sash
*outfit on right is from Colleen Thompson

9070 – Lassie Coat
Blue wool coat w/ white linen collar, 3 white buttons, hat & signature purse; (has also been seen rarely in red as this one such as this one from Colleen Thompson); Lassie was also a brand for human clothing in the 50's.

| 9103 & 9172 – Bridal Costume Satin gown w/ tulle over-skirt, lace over satin bodice on 9103; **tulle over satin bodice on 9172**, long sleeves & scoop neck; tulle veil with gathers at one end (probably without bow), flower bouquet which is missing in photo | Here is a comparison of the 4 Little Miss Revlon brides: from left 9364; 9170; 9103/9172; 9040 |

9104 & 9160 - Taffeta Formal
Net overskirt, lace over taffeta bodice, taffeta waist sash/bow, stockings; came in pale pink, powder blue & lavender

**This is one of several outfits that had 2 style numbers. It is generally accepted that style numbers indicate what year they were sold (i.e. 90 series in 1957, 91 series in '58, etc) so most likely when outfits had 2 different style numbers it is due to their being re-released under the second number.

9105 – Torso Dress
Cotton dress w/ 3 rhinestones
on boat-neck collar + crinoline
Came in:
Aqua paisley
Aqua bugs print
Pink & aqua daisies
Blue flowers
Aqua floral stripes
Pink hearts
Red/white/blue plaid
Green plaid

9105 - Torso dress
from Pat Derelanko

9105 - Torso dress
from the collection of Gail
Gavit

25

9109 - Bow Dress
Green stripes on white dress w/ brown bow; or pink on white
w/ purple bow

9114 -School Dress
Solid color dress w/ print across bodice & sleeves + crinoline - came in yellow w/ several print top
versions, blue w/ white/pink print top, pink yoke version & lime green w/ print top

9115 - Polka Dot Dress
Cotton dress w/ white polka dots,
fluffy loop trim, crinoline - came in
red, hot pink, aqua & blue
*The doll in the red dress is my sister's
childhood doll that never got played
with – I rescued her from the bottom
of a closet recently, restored her &
she now has a valued place in my
sister's household – We think she
looks a lot like Lucille Ball in the era of
"I Love Lucy" & resides with her Lucy
collection

9116 - Calypso Blouse and Skirt
Yellow or white bodysuit blouse
(white shirt w/ ruffle trim, or
yellow shirt w/ multicolor rick-
rack); solid blue or black floral
skirt w/ various rick-rack trims;
red trimmed crinoline

9118 - Traveling Outfit
Gold cotton dress w/
orange dots, aqua rick-
rack, + crinoline w/ aqua
trim & felt hat w/ pear

9117 - Visiting Outfit
Cotton dress w/ bright striped skirt,
white pique top w/ red snaps, red
edged crinoline, red hat w/ red veil,
attached red vinyl belt - has sometimes
been seen with a matching striped rain
coat & tote

Ruffled crinolines that
came with colored edges:
Princess – pink & blue
Sunday - black
Traveling – aqua
Calypso – red

9119 – Jumper
Blue dress w/ attached white organdy blouse, pink rick-rack trim + crinoline - came in 2 styles of short sleeves *dress on right is from Pat Derelanko

9120 - Striped Dress - Vertically striped cotton dress, red purse, crinoline, stockings – Came in 3 red/white versions (wide or narrow stripes, different placement of rick-rack) & navy/white version

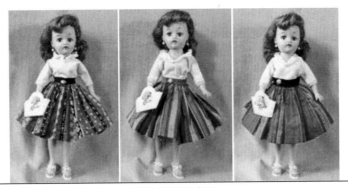

9121 - Gay Stripe Dress
Bright multicolor striped skirt, white pique V-neck top, white signature purse, crinoline, stockings; skirt came in 3 different prints

9122 - Party Dress
Red taffeta dress w/ silver edging, rhinestone @ center front, white purse & stockings **a similar dress (see right) in red/white check, or pink/white check taffeta w/ white trim but no rhinestone & different sleeves has been determined to be a different unknown style number

9123 - School Dress
Cotton dress w/ white collar, black grosgrain tie, purse, stockings – came in coral, aqua, blue or yellow w/ white stripes; yellow, lime or pink w/ white dots; chartreuse green w/ black geometric shapes

9126 - Pinafore
White sheer pinafore attached to red print dress + purse & stockings

9127 - Pinafore
Sheer print pinafore over solid lavender dress or sheer embroidered white pinafore over red print dress + purse & stockings

9130 - Sailor Outfit
Navy blue cotton dress w/ red & white trim, blue on white embroidered hanky @ waist, white hat w/ red bias trim, crinoline - also came in a denim-like fabric version w/ square sew-on snaps & red on white embroidered hanky @ waist

9131 - Pink Print Dress
Solid dark pink bodice w/ white rick-rack trim & pink print skirt

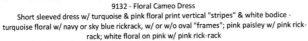

9132 - Floral Cameo Dress
Short sleeved dress w/ turquoise & pink floral print vertical "stripes" & white bodice - turquoise floral w/ navy or sky blue rickrack, w/ or w/o oval "frames"; pink paisley w/ pink rick-rack; white floral on pink w/ pink rick-rack

9135 - Raincoat
Short white vinyl raincoat w/ standup collar, 3 red horizontal attachments w/ 2 white snaps on each end

9141 - Sunday Outfit
Polished cotton dress w/ yellow/gray striped skirt & sleeves, gray bodice, black straw hat w/ black veil, black edged crinoline

Purse & hat that came with princess outfits

9142 - Princess Style Outfit - Taffeta dress w/ checked, wide or narrow striped pattern on mid-calf length circle skirt, blue velvet bow trim, pink/blue edged crinoline, pink/blue straw hat w/ pink veil, blue felt purse w/ flowers

9143 - Velvet Sheath
Black velvet sleeveless dress w/ 3/4 sleeve white sheer gauzy blouse, white veiled hat, black velvet purse w/ attached flowers
(note purse is same style as princess purse but black instead of blue)

9156 - Ball Gown w/ attached shawl
Taffeta & net gown w/ V neckline & attached net shawl - red, rose, light blue, yellow, pink or aqua

9157 - Lace Formal
Aqua blue taffeta gown w/
black lace overskirt, flowers
in hair, stockings

9158 - Nylon Formal
Rose taffeta gown w/
sheer flocked overskirt,
diagonal floral band,
stockings (these flowers
were replaced)

9159 - Debutante Gown
White & silver striped skirt (3
versions) w/ short black lace
overskirt + flowers, long, black-
edged crinoline

9160 - Taffeta Formal (also sold as style #9104)
Net overskirt, lace over taffeta bodice, taffeta waist sash/bow, stockings - came in pale pink, powder blue & lavender

 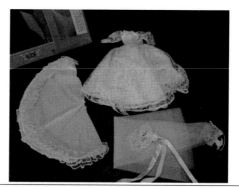

9170 – Debutante Bridal Gown
Lace gown over embossed taffeta w/ high neck, long sleeves, solid raglan under-bodice, 2 long lace pieces @ waist -
2 versions - all lace or w/ some satin - also 2 versions of taffeta underskirt + flowers, pearls around neck, crinoline;
*boxed outfit on right has never been on a doll, from Katherine Beier

9171- Bridesmaid Outfit
Pink satin gown w/ 3 tier tulle overskirt, drop shoulder satin bodice, + large horsehair patio hat, flowers, stockings

9176 – Hostess Gown
Pink gown & net robe w/ lace, blue tie + mirror + pink shoes

9177 – Shorty Nightgown
2 piece print short gown & matching panties w/ white lace
- Came in red or blue floral print w/ green leaves on white cotton, or pale pink flowers on sheer fabric

9178 - Pajamas Cotton PJ's w/ long pants/short sleeves, rounded yoke on top, white lace trim - Came in blue, pink, or yellow floral print; red/white/blue plaid

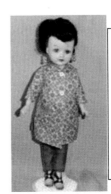

9179 - Lounging Pajamas Long blue print silky top & solid royal blue cotton pants w/ elastic waist; also a rare version has been seen, possibly one-of-a-kind, black w/ pink flowered top & solid pink pants

9204 - Coolie Beach Outfit Red oriental print sunsuit, matching jacket, coolie hat w/ red serged edge, paper parasol *from Colleen Thompson's collection *Also came in a dark blue version

9205 - Coolie Beach Outfit Red floral print sunsuit, matching jacket, coolie hat w/ red bias trim, red sunglasses, red shoes

 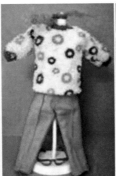 

9207 - TV Lounging Outfit
Gold corduroy pants, green/gold/white or red/green/white diamond print terrycloth top, green net scarf & red glasses; or white/red/green/gold circle design top
*Circle top outfit is from Pat Derelanko
*version on right is from Colleen Thompson

9208 - Pedal Pusher Outfit
Woven cotton pedal pushers
& red knit top + red sun
glasses - pants came in
red/black/white plaid, dark
red/navy/white plaid, or
lighter white/navy/red plaid

9209 - Jeans and Shirt
Blue denim jeans, red/white striped or checked
shirt + rigid plastic bowler hat
*see below for the 2 hat versions to this outfit
*hat also has been found in pink

9210 - Skirt & Blouse
Print skirt & solid color blouse + stockings, black purse - red or aqua print
skirt w/ yellow 3/4 sleeve blouse or short sleeve white blouse
*outfit on right is from Leslie Aiken

9211 - Sunsuit
Short cotton strapless body suit with tie-on skirt + coolie hat - blue/white stripe,
pink/white stripe, pink or blue w/ black butterfly print

9212 – Sweater & Skirt Outfit
Felt skirt & knit top, purse, stockings - purple skirt w/ butterfly & pink top; navy skirt w/ pink
butterfly & yellow top; navy skirt w/ red top; tan skirt w/ butterfly & white top; red skirt w/
black bow & gold top; [also red skirt w/ black scotty dog & white top which might not be
LMR]
*skirts & top on right from Colleen Thompson

9213 - Red Print Jumper
Red print jumper & white gauzy
short sleeved blouse
- 2 different red print versions

9215 – 2 Piece Play Suit
Royal blue cotton Bermuda
shorts & red fold-over
blouse w/ blue rick-rack &
no snap

9216 - Sun Dress & Bonnet
Halter style print dress & matching bonnet w/ bias binding trim - 2 red f
print versions w/ yellow trim, red stripe print w/ yellow trim, or blue p
version

9240 - Checked Coat, Hat &
Purse
Black & white flared hounds-
tooth coat w/ 5 black buttons,
or 1 white snap, or 3 white
snaps w/ red/gold trim, + red
flexible straw hat & red
signature purse

9218 - 2 Piece Pajama
Short sleeve flared top & solid red capri pants - tops came in red
floral, red geometric print or red stars

9241 - Flared Woolen Coat
Flared fleece open coat - white, red, dark blue, yellow, tan, or purple

9249 - Negligee Set
Pink lace robe w/ net long sleeves, net ruffle @ neck
& gathered wrists, satin ribbon ties @neck & wrists;
taffeta gown w/ satin bows on shoulders, net trim
around neckline & satin ribbon tie waist, snap
closure in back; 3 pink rubber curlers

This style is very likely #9251 - 2 piece cotton dress with tie
at waist of top - recently found in a box with this number -
previously this outfit had an unknown style number &
boxes with this number had unknown styles in them
*dress on right from Colleen Thompson has a very rare
light blue version signature purse

9252 - Raincoat, Boots, Tote Bag
Polished cotton hooded coat + clear boots & tote bag - came in white w/aqua or red dots, yellow w/ multicolor dots, aqua w/ white dots, blue w/ white dots (matches dress #0821) or multicolor dots, pale blue or pink w/ multicolor "x"s, aqua or orange w/ white stars (w/ or w/o matching dress), or white w/ navy or red stars (sorry, most of these are missing boots & tote)

I put paper inside this tote so it could be seen better & hung it with a string from her wrist

9254 - 5-pc Striped Suit
Navy w/ red trim flared coat (3 fabric versions), gold bead on each lapel; mid-calf length skirt w/ attached red plastic belt, slit in back, snap closure; white long sleeve bodysuit w/ lace around neck, down the front in 2 rows, & on sleeve edges, or red cotton knit long sleeved top; navy blue felt hat w/ red feather, red purse, & red shoes + cameo necklace (cameos here are replacements)

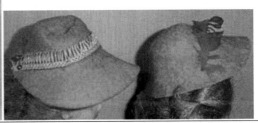

9255 - 5-pc Redingote Outfit

Straight blue coat, lined with polka dot fabric; red polka dot skirt w/ snap back closure; scarf w/ pearl stick pin (laps over under coat – this is the only top); red purse; red belt; red felt hat w/ aqua plastic fringe as hatband, or feather & cross pin (authenticity of this feather hat version has been controversial)

9256 - Nurse Outfit

Blue dress, white pinafore apron & nurse cap w/ dark navy stripe or red cross + stockings

9257 - Artist's Outfit

Flared smock style cotton top w/ paint smudges, black capri pants, red beret, shoes, palette & brush - tops came in pink, yellow, or off white (2 versions of the palette are shown here)

9280 - Crinoline (set of 2)
2 fancy crinolines w/ extra net ruffles around hem -one pink w/ white trim, one white w/ pink trim

9258 - Ballerina Outfit
Blue or white tutu, flowers in hair & matching heels

9284 - Shoes & Stockings
2 pair each in clear "hat box"

9286 - Hangers
Set of 6 in assorted colors

9287 - Hat in Hatbox
Came in assorted colors, usually with a veil

*from Katherine Beier

9285 - Eyeglasses
one pair in assorted colors

9299 - Little Miss Revlon doll Stand
Beige plastic base & upright flattened tube with etched Ideal logo in base, uncoated silver tone wire

9289 - Little Miss Revlon Travel Case
Black or blue vinyl case w/ window over left half, Little Miss Revlon signature on right side, swivel latch on top, molded plastic compartments + hanger rod & drawer inside; also pictured in white in LMR catalog but that version was probably never produced

9350 – 2 piece Cotton Sleeping Outfit
Cotton print PJ's w/ short sleeve, high-waisted top & long pants - yellow, pink or blue floral stripe, or red polka dots on white

9351 – Percale School Dress
V-neck dress in blue (2 prints), green, gold, or red (3 prints) w/ white/black print & black rick-rack + panty *right dress from Colleen Thompson

9352 - Trench Coat
Tan vinyl trench coat, triangle scarf, belt, metal rings & snaps, & tote

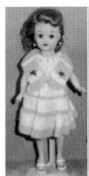

9353 - Knit Dress
Knit yarn dress w/
horizontal stripes, seed
pearls around neckline;
matching stole + petticoat
& purse; came in
yellow/white, red/white,
pink/white, or blue/white

9354 - Strapless Print Percale
Dress
Blue & green cotton print
strapless dress w/ net overskirt
(or rarely, lace such as version on
right) + panty

9355 - 2 piece Shirtwaist
Dress
Checked w/ straw hat &
matching hatband, white
belt, white purse - came
in blue/white,
aqua/white, lilac/white
or pink/white checks; or
in purple/white stripe
*trio photo is from
Katherine Beier

9356 - Play Outfit
Print or plaid capri pants w/ solid white or colored crop top & long matching sash around waist + straw hat -
blue vine print, green stripe print, red tulip print, blue floral print, turquoise plaid
-2 outfits on right are from Colleen Thompson

9358 - Blue Taffeta Cocktail Suit
Checked or solid taffeta skirt w/ gold elastic waist,
solid taffeta bolero jacket, white sheer dotted Swiss
blouse, red satin hat, red shoes, red purse, stockings -
came in navy blue & black versions

9357 - Strapless Taffeta
Party Dress Solid navy or
burgundy taffeta dress
w/ white lace trimmed,
drop shoulder collar +
panty

9359 - Velvet & Nylon
Party Dress
White flocked nylon
skirt w/ stamped design
& velvet edging @ hem
to match bodice, velvet
long sleeved top,
flowered headband hat,
purse, crinoline,
stockings - Came in
red/white or
royal/white - red/white
dress & hat close-up
from Colleen Thompson

9360 - Ice Skating Outfit
Leopard flannel skirt & headband, red bodysuit, black tights & white skates w/ red trim
*closeup of headband is the underside showing the wire running down the center

9361-7 - Velvet Flared Coat
Velvet coat w/ 1 white snap, white fur muff, hat - solid red, aqua, green or royal blue

Little Miss Revlon Signature Purses + others that have been found with outfits (there was also a light blue version signature purse - see #9251) from Colleen Thompson

9362 - Black Net Formal
Aqua blue satin bell skirt w/ 2 layer black net overskirt, 3 horizontal aqua ribbons on skirt, matching net/ribbon stole, flower corsage @ waist, petticoat

9364 - Bridal Outfit
Long lace sleeves w/ zig-zag placed gold or silver rick-rack (or lace version) on skirt, veil w/ tiara, petticoat, flowers, stockings

9363 - Bridesmaid Outfit
Short sleeve pink taffeta & net gown w/ ruffled high neck, pink/gold rick-rack @ neck, hem of underskirt & on net ruffle mid-way up overskirt; wide circle hat which is the same as 9171 bridesmaid; crinoline; flower bouquet

Close-up of the bridesmaid hat for style #s 9171 & 9363

9364 Bridal
without metallic rick-rack
*from Gail Gavit

9420 - Rick-Rack Dress
Cotton school dress w/ wide white hem & yellow rick-rack
*dress on right from Colleen Thompson

9421 - Blue Denim Outfit
Blue denim skirt w/ red checked shirt + red shoes

9422 - Cotton Print Dress & Stole
Solid pink, aqua or white dress w/ diagonal fabric
trim & matching stole - trims came in several color
combo stripes, rose/green elliptical shapes or
chartreuse/rose diamonds – outfit on right from
Colleen Thompson

9425 - Cotton Check Bolero Outfit
Aqua/white check strapless dress & bolero jacket w/ black
rick rack & black lacy open-circle hat, flowers, attached
crinoline, signature purse – dress is missing flowers at waist
– hat is the same as 9037 orange dress except this one has
flowers
*hat is from Colleen Thompson

9427 - Felt Coat Outfit
Black coat w/ red print knit
collar, 5 snaps, matching black
felt pillbox hat w/ daisy
appliques, red purse – matches
red/white knit dress 9024

9431 - Velvet Cocktail Suit
Strapless dress w/ white lace bodice extending to front strip on teal velvet skirt ; teal velvet bolero jacket & hat w/ lace on crown + stockings & purse

9432 - Red Stripe Formal
Red/white stripe skirt w/ black velvet & white cotton bodice, daisies, stockings - also came in a checked skirt version

The following have unknown style numbers but most are believed to be genuine Ideal-made

*other researchers have more information on style numbers so stay tuned, the work continues

Taffeta Dropped Waist Dress - has 3 rhinestones on right shoulder; tagged

2 piece dress – print top with solid color sleeves, shoulders & back, one snap in back at neckline, rick rack trim; wrap skirt of same fabric with solid color waistband & one snap at waist, rick rack trim; tagged

Aqua & Silver Party Dress – Short sleeve dress of semi-sheer aqua & metallic silver, fitted bodice with a square neckline & a rhinestone in each corner, V-shaped back with 2 snaps, attached white net crinoline; tagged

Aqua dress is style #0821 which is believed to be a Crown Princess style – came with matching panties

*Raincoat is LMR #9252

48

Taffeta Bubble Dress
One shoulder style cocktail dress made of iridescent taffeta; skirt is gathered underneath & attached to lining that attaches to waistline which gives the ballooning effect; flowers at waist, two snaps in back; tagged

Cotton school dress
Blue & white striped dress w/ white lace vertical trim on bodice, white rick rack around neck & black grosgrain ribbon "tie", 2 snap closure in back; tagged; can be seen in the 1958 Spiegel catalog

Lantern House Dress
Long sleeve, mid-calf length dress in cotton lantern & star print, bodice trimmed with white lace & red piping, single snap at waist; tagged

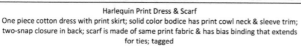

Harlequin Print Dress & Scarf
One piece cotton dress with print skirt; solid color bodice has print cowl neck & sleeve trim; two-snap closure in back; scarf is made of same print fabric & has bias binding that extends for ties; tagged

Navy Nylon Dress
Red print on navy, red velvet ribbon, white flocked hearts, attached white taffeta half-slip —untagged, but believed to be a Crown Princess dress

Green Striped School Dress
Has red rick rack trim around
neck & in V formation on
bodice, 2 snap closure in
back – from Pat Derelanko;
tagged

Plaid Taffeta dresses with picot trimmed braid Dress on left was found in my gift
set - these are now believed to be Crown Princess dresses, although untagged

Dress & Coat outfit
from Theriault's
Tonner auction

Faux Leather Coat & Tote
Although untagged, I am almost
certain this set is genuine Ideal –
identical to 20inch doll size set
*from Colleen Thompson

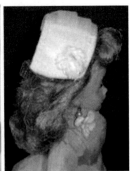

Faille Coat & Hat – untagged but both pieces are identical to larger Revlon doll coat
sets – note flowers on shoulder & same flowers on hats *coat in center from
Katherine Beier
*the hat on right has tulle over the faille, all of which is pleated

Very unusual LMR brocade outfit identical to the one on the right which is on a 17 inch doll and is from Kathy Barna's book "Revlon Dolls and Their Look-alikes". The LMR outfit hem is done with the Revlon trademark. Net is doubled and used to finish the hem and also the gauntlets. The bustle snaps on with two snaps (grommet type) like ones used on some other Revlon clothing.

Animal print taffeta party dresses – untagged – probably not Ideal

Known style numbers with unknown appearance
The following style numbers are known to exist (empty boxes have been found with these numbers stamped on them) but we haven't been able to determine what was in the boxes: 9020, 9100, 9101, 9108, 9110, 9111, 9133, 9200, 9202, 9203, 9230, 9250, 9253, 9335. Also 9426 is known to be a pedal pusher outfit but not what it looks like. The same is true for 9430 which is known to be a beatnik outfit but not what it looks like. I hope these mysteries are solved in my lifetime – I will certainly keep trying.

There are many more outfits that fit Little Miss Revlon but have either been ruled out as Ideal-made or are too uncertain & untagged to be included in this document. There are also outfits identified by other collectors which aren't included here. Most of my research of the past 25 years has been focused on this quest & will continue, but new information & questions have slowed down enough that it seemed like a good time to publish what we have learned to date.

**See Judith Izen's "Ideal Dolls" books for several original outfits that are not included in this document (both for Little Miss Revlon & the larger dolls). One of the most important is on page #157 of her 3rd edition which may be style #0930 Glamour Gown described in the Ideal catalog as "strapless taffeta with petal skirt, short cape and gauntlets".
In 2nd edition is #9174 Plaid Pajamas.
in 2nd edition is a photo of the cross hat version for the LMR #9256 Nurse.
In 2nd edition a Checked Coat, hat & unusual purse #9240.
In 2nd & 3rd editions is a 15" doll outfit with leaf print bodice, brown skirt & hat which was sold separately.

Larger Revlon Doll Outfits

Kissing Pink styles – lowest cost of the 3 original styles & named after Revlon lipstick color, as were many of the outfits
*these styles came with pearl jewelry & no hats

Kissing Pink Striped Cotton Dresses in 15", 18", 20" & 22"
These stripes are ¼" wide & these are the sizes in which this dress was made *other color versions were bright yellow & salmon (note the tan dress version which has a square neck & 3/8" wide stripe); the waist seam is below the waist of the doll, there is a rhinestone stud at the bottom of the bow tab *15" size has a grosgrain ribbon bow; multiple snap closure in back of 3 or 4 depending on the size of doll

This dress is from the Theriault's Tonner auction
*note the diamond box which was the earliest box sold

Note the square neckline & wider stripes on this cotton striped Kissing Pink dress
*this version also came in a salmon color

Kissing Pink square neck taffeta dresses – came in blue, pale yellow, aqua, & dusty pink – pictured are all 18" size but these dresses were also made for 20" & 22"
*from Gail Gavit

Kissing Pink cotton dresses for 15 inch with dropped waist, bias organza boat neck collars & hem trim – these boat neck dresses have a low V in the back & a 2 snap closure; bodices were cut on the bias & have center front seams

This lavender & aqua style came in 15" & 18" sizes

rear view of boat neck style

Kissing Pink nylon boat neck Butterfly Dresses in 2 color versions

More Kissing Pink versions for 15 inch dolls

Kissing Pink Linen Dresses – Have grosgrain ribbon & cummerbund type styling at waist – came in colors as shown in 18", 20" & 22" sizes *the ash blond hair color is extremely unusual

Kissing Pink Heart Dresses
- Above 3 dresses are taffeta – middle dress has oxidized from original navy blue color & right dress has oxidized from original red
- Below 2 dresses are nylon – these dresses came on 18", 20" & 22" dolls *note bodices on nylon dresses had no hearts in fabric
- Brown nylon dress was navy blue originally

Kissing Pink Jacket Dresses – dresses are woven cotton & jackets are cotton knit with dress fabric on collar – some also had woven fabric facings – also came in a green version - came in 18" & 20" sizes

20" dress without jacket

This charming trio is from Katherine Beier

Cherries a la Mode styles – middle priced of the 3 original styles & again named after a Revlon lipstick color

Accessories included pearl earrings, graduated pearl necklaces & hats, except for 15" size which had no hats

15" size Cherries a la Mode dresses came with only wrap-around snake style necklaces & no hats
*On the larger dolls (3rd from left), note the difference in flower color on the hats

This pink floral version of Cherries a la Mode came in 18", 20" & 22" as pictured *doll on the left is my childhood doll

Rare taffeta dress from Theriault's Tonner auction *also came in an aqua version

These light blue & yellow versions are very rare

Cherries a la Mode taffeta dress with lace bodice inset
*has sometimes been found on dolls with side part hairstyles
*has also been found in a pink version
*green version above from Theriault's Tonner auction

Cherries a la Mode Eyelet versions in blue & pink – taffeta underskirts & bodices
*came in 18", 20" & 22" sizes

Cherries a la Mode Flocked Dresses in navy & pink – came in 18", 20" & rarely 22" sizes

Cherries a la Mode Dotted Swiss Dresses – middle dress from Nancy Moustoukkis; right dress from Robert Tonner's 2010 UFDC convention exhibit

Queen of Diamonds – highest priced outfits of the 3 original styles
Outfits often included rhinestone earrings, necklaces & rings + rabbit fur stoles

Queen of Diamonds Velveteen Dresses in all the original colors *from Katherine Beier

Queen of Diamonds rhinestone jewelry – other versions of the necklace & earrings have been found but these are the most common

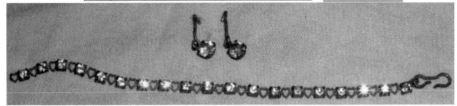

Queen of Diamonds Coat Dress Outfits sold by Sears – 3 on left from Katherine Beier
*Blue version on right from Robert Tonner's 2010 UFDC exhibit & worn by an extremely rare high color 22" doll

Queen of Diamonds Brocade Dresses with tulle sleeves, upper bodice & tie belts – also came in a red version
*made in 18", 20" & 22" sizes

Queen of Diamonds Tiered Lace Dresses with tulle sleeves & edging of the lace tiers, satin bow at waist *came in 18", 20"& 22" sizes

Queen of Diamonds Chintz Dresses in 22" size – came with rhinestone necklace, earrings & ring + a plastic brooch
*has also been seen in yellow on an 18" doll

Back view of the chintz dress & close-up of the pin that came on the chintz dresses

Snow Pink on walker doll *see close-up of shoulders for detail of pleated construction

Evening Star outfit - sold by Sears, 1957 – dress is taffeta with gold threads & belt; coat is velvet with fur trim, lined with satin; came with Queen of Diamonds accessories (rhinestone earrings, necklace & ring)
*According to the catalog the outfit was made for 18" walking dolls but this coat fits a 20" doll better

Gowns

Deb doll & her gowns – these dolls & gowns are 17-18" size but Deb dolls in teddies were also sold in 15" & 20" in 1960

These 2 gowns from Theriault's
Tonner auction

From Nancy
Moustoukkis

Gowns above courtesy of Theriault's from Tonner auction

2 additional Deb gowns

These 2 taffeta, lace & tulle gowns are identical (LMR version is #9160)

"Swirling Formal" gowns - these gowns were sold by
Montgomery Wards – bodices came in several
different colors

These gowns were sold by
Sears as "Happi- Time"
walker dolls, which were not
actual Ideal Revlon dolls,
didn't have the usual
markings but were made the
same; outfits were tagged
"Idea"; also came in a pink
version * blue version here is
from Gail Gavit

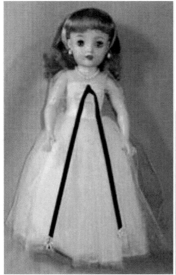

Pants Outfits

20 inch Bendable Knee 5th Avenue dolls & outfits
Unlined velour jackets, cotton knit body suits & woven cotton pants with side snap opening

Outfit on left has a replaced jacket & outfit on the right has a replaced bodysuit *often these outfits are found without jackets since that piece hasn't held up over time as well as the other pieces in the outfit *I have never seen the teardrop print pants in a complete original outfit nor anywhere else by themselves

This photo is from Theriault's Tonner auction & shows how the dolls were boxed

closeup of bodysuit that goes with paisley pants outfit

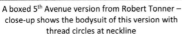

A boxed 5th Avenue version from Robert Tonner – close-up shows the bodysuit of this version with thread circles at neckline

2 straight leg dolls in pants outfits – very rare & possibly one of a kind – from Theriault's Tonner auction & now in Katherine Beier's collection

Brides

Snow Peach Brides in 22" & 18" sizes – also came in 20" size – from Theriault's Tonner auction	22" Glamour Bride from Katherine Beier -style #0927 *headpiece is a vintage-style replacement	Rare 18 inch bride from Robert Tonner

Outfits sold separately

In addition to the Deb doll gowns there were a few outfits sold separately by Ideal, mostly for 18" doll size

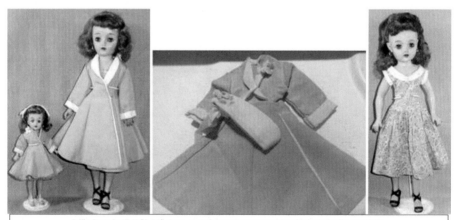

Faille Coats in 10 ½ "& 20" sizes – note hats are constructed with pleated tulle over faille
*This dress was sold with the faille coat outfit & there was also a red version of the dress which can be seen in Kathy Barna's book

Faux Leather
Coat in 20" size -
Identical to 10 ½"
size on page 39

Halter Dress in 10 ½" & 18" sizes with – top is velveteen with
gold edging; skirt is polished cotton with gold highlights
*photo on right from Theriault's Tonner auction

18 inch Delightful Organdy in 3 versions - has velvet tie belt

These 18inch cotton dresses were named 7R2

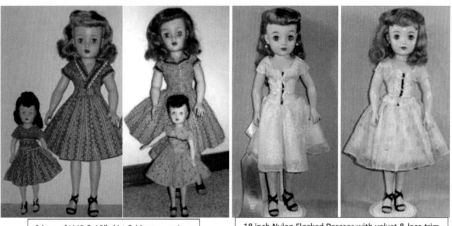

*duos of LMR & 18" skirt & blouse versions
from Nancy Moustoukkis

18 inch Nylon Flocked Dresses with velvet & lace trim

Late Production dolls & outfits

Toward the end of the 1950s Ideal was struggling to compete in the doll market & changed the Revlon dolls to a lower quality vinyl & dressed these dolls in lower quality outfits. The VT18 & VT20 marks are still present but the dolls are actually 17" & 19" tall. Outfits are all believed to be not tagged. See Kathy Barna's "Revlon Dolls & their Look-Alikes" for several other examples.

Doll on left from Nancy Moustoukkis
*note the large eyes & different face mold that was often present in late production dolls

This 17 inch doll was sold by Sears in 1961 & marketed as "the Slender Doll"

Another 17 inch late production doll

Possibly one of a kind 22" high color doll in skirt outfit – acrylic skirt has red knit lining – velvet jacket – red knit bodysuit – gold elastic head band – pearl jewelry *because the skirt is shorter than the style of the day & the jacket is extremely tight, it may have been intended for a shorter doll *from Katherine Beier

Early production doll

In 1956, Ideal sold a 20 inch doll that had very heavy arms *doll on the right is from Theriault's Tonner auction, now in Katherine Beier's collection *the pink dress is taffeta, the green is faille; both have attached slips
*the gold version is from Nancy Moustoukkis
*below is rear view of the 2 dresses above

Glamour Dolls & Gowns – style numbers according to 1958 Ideal catalog

#0921 in two color versions on 22" dolls *from Katherine Beier

#0933 on 25"; #0929 on 22"
*from Katherine Beier

Style #0932 on 25" doll
(would be style #0922
on a 22" doll)
* the gem of my
collection

#0927 on 22" doll
*from Katherine Beier

#0924 on 22" doll *from
Katherine Beier

22" side part doll in Glamour Gown
style #9026 (probably)
Brown lace over yellow taffeta *note
unusual hair style
*from Sandy Herman

Hair & Bodies

Pixie cut doll – very
rare

Side part doll often
found with
Cherries a la Mode
taffeta dress with
lace insert bodice
(see pg 48)

Most common Miss Revlon hairstyle, especially
with Queen of Diamonds outfits but often with
all larger Revlon dolls

Rare doll with widow's peak
*from Robert Tonner

The four faces of 18" dolls
*from Kathy Barna's "Revlon Dolls
and their Look-alikes"

Pixie faced dolls & their lower
quality outfits that were sold late
in the Revlon production period
*from Kathy Barna's "Revlon Dolls
and their Look-alikes"

This shows the internal structure
of *some* larger Revlon dolls (no
wonder these dolls have held up
so well for 60+ years); it also
shows how some dolls had
painted parts; I believe these
tended to be early in the
production period

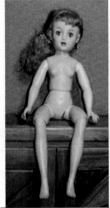

Bendable Knee doll
showing knee structure;
occasionally the lower
parts of the legs on these
dolls have faded to nearly
white & in some cases
only one leg has this
condition; rarely some of
the bendable knee dolls
are also walkers;
additionally this shows
the side pony tail hairstyle
of the bendable knee
dolls

Walker doll
showing the
button indicating
the walker
mechanism is
present
(Does not need
to be pushed for
the mechanism
to be
operational)

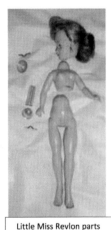

Little Miss Revlon parts
*the most commonly
missing part is the torso
tube which falls out when
the doll comes apart, but
which can be easily be
replaced with a piece of
pvc tubing *I recommend
1/16" covered cording for
restringing

Accessories

Shoes

Little Miss Revlon shoes
-there are several versions of plastic shoes here from that era, some of which may not be genuine Ideal but one thing for certain, Little Miss Revlon <u>never</u> came in crisscross elastic shoes like her bigger sisters *all of these (1-4) came in many colors

1 - This style has been found on both LMR & larger dolls

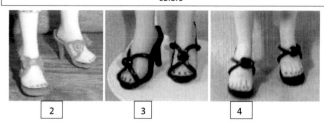

Miss Revlon shoes – the crisscross elastic style is by far the most common & came in gold (on glamour dolls & 5th Avenue dolls) & white (on brides) in addition to black; the black plastic version(7) came on some of the later release dolls; the bottom versions (8 & 9) were common styles for 15" dolls – came in several colors

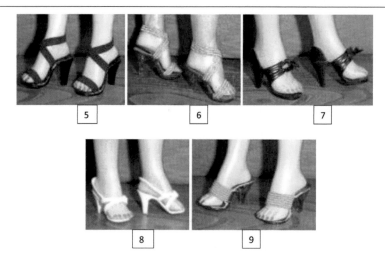

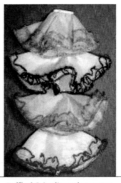

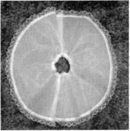

Little Miss Revlon panties & crinoline that came with some outfits

Ruffled Crinolines that came
with some LMR outfits
#9142 Princess – pink & blue
#9141 Sunday - black
#9118 Traveling – aqua
#9116 Calypso – red

Miss Revlon panties & petticoat that came with most outfits; exceptions are:
*Cherries a la Mode navy cherries version that had a navy petticoat that has usually oxidized to dark red now
*brides that had white panties & petticoats
*5th Avenue outfits & swimsuit slender doll that had no panties
*a few outfits that had attached petticoats
*note when these garments have lost their crispness, several layers of spray starch, smoothing & straightening the tiers between sprays/drying (not pressing) helps to bring them back to life

Pearl jewelry that was worn by most Miss Revlon dolls except Queen of Diamonds & most Glamour dolls *note that earring posts are bent over at the ends so they don't slip out after being inserted into the dolls' ears – this is also why they should never be just pulled out of the doll - the ear hole will rip
*2 round necklaces above are known as "snake" type & the one to the left above is known as "graduated" *both types came in different sizes depending on the size of the doll

Straw hat worn on Cherries a la Mode dolls – color of flowers varied

Tag that was sewn into the waistband of many Miss Revlon larger doll outfits (& often removed by the new owner)

Boxes

The earliest doll boxes were diamond pattern followed by pictures of the dolls on the covers

The gold box + the 3 boxes on the right are Little Miss Revlon outfit boxes

Catalogs & Ads

Ideal 1956

Ideal catalogs were sent to retailers for pre-ordering store stock

Often, depending on the amount of interest by buyers, some items were not subsequently produced or produced in small quantities

*The three 5th Avenue dolls in the 1958 catalog are examples of this. The dolls were produced but sold by Sears with different hair styles & different pants outfits

*25" dolls were never pictured in the Ideal catalogs

KISSING PINK (pearl necklace)				CHERRIES A LA MODE (hat, pearl necklace and earrings)				QUEEN OF DIAMONDS (fur stole, rhinestone necklace, earrings and ring)			
NO.	SIZE	PACKED	LBS. RETAIL	NO.	SIZE	PACKED	LBS. RETAIL	NO.	SIZE	PACKED	LBS. RETAIL
0940	18"	⅓ doz.	14 12.00	0945	18"	⅓ doz.	14 14.00	0950	18"	⅓ doz.	14 16.00
0960	20"	⅓ doz.	10 16.00	0965	20"	⅓ doz.	10 18.00	0970	20"	⅓ doz.	10 20.00
0980	23"	¼ doz.	12 20.00	0985	23"	¼ doz.	12 22.00	0990	23"	¼ doz.	12 25.00

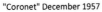

"Coronet" December 1957

Ideal 1957

Ideal 1958 *I have never seen the pants styles above except in these photos so they may not have been produced

The beautiful Revlon Snow Peach Bride

Snow Peach Bride

In breathtaking floor length bridal gown, long-sleeved and jewel-necked. With delicate lace bodice and lace overlay skirt. Floor length tulle bridal veil trimmed in lace with crown set off with orange blossoms. Holds wedding bouquet with trailing white satin streamers. With teardrop pearl earrings and necklace and ring.

NO.	SIZE	PACKED	WEIGHT
0855	18"	½ doz	14 lbs
0875	20"	½ doz	10 lbs
0895	23"	½ doz	12 lbs

Ideal 1958

Revlon Glamour doll

The glamorous Revlon Doll is more glamorous than ever, ready for her gala evening in the very height of fashion. She wears appropriate earrings, necklace and ring to complement these exquisite creations.

NO.	SIZE	DESCRIPTION	WEIGHT
0921	23"	Net and Lace Dress w/Matching Stole	
0922	23"	Strapless Gown w/Tiers of Ruffles	4 lbs
0923	23"	Velvet Dress—w/Lace	4 lbs
0924	23"	Velvet Ball Gown w/Lace Sideaweep	4 lbs
0925	23"	Velvet Dress w/Tulle Side Panel	4 lbs
0926	23"	Lace over Taffeta w/Long Sleeves	4 lbs
0927	23"	Bride	4 lbs
0928	23"	Taffeta Dress w/Net Side Panel	4 lbs
0929	23"	Navy Dress w/Lace Trim	4 lbs
0930	23"	Strapless Taffeta w/Petal Skirt, Short Cape & Gauntlets to Match	4 lbs
0931	26"	Net and Lace Dress w/Matching Stole	5 lbs
0932	26"	Strapless Gown w/Tiers of Ruffles	5 lbs
0939	26"	Navy Dress w/Lace Trim	5 lbs

Individually packed

Revlon Glamour doll

The glamorous Revlon Doll is more glamorous than ever, ready for her gala evening in the very height of fashion. She wears appropriate earrings, necklace and ring to complement these exquisite creations.

NO.	SIZE	DESCRIPTION	WEIGHT
0921	23"	Net and Lace Dress w/Matching Stole	
0922	23"	Strapless Gown w/Tiers of Ruffles	4 lbs
0923	23"	Velvet Dress—w/Lace	4 lbs
0924	23"	Velvet Ball Gown w/Lace Sideaweep	4 lbs
0925	23"	Velvet Dress w/Tulle Side Panel	4 lbs
0926	23"	Lace over Taffeta w/Long Sleeves	4 lbs
0927	23"	Bride	4 lbs
0928	23"	Taffeta Dress w/Net Side Panel	4 lbs
0929	23"	Navy Dress w/Lace Trim	4 lbs
0930	23"	Strapless Taffeta w/Petal Skirt, Short Cape & Gauntlets to Match	4 lbs
0931	26"	Net and Lace Dress w/Matching Stole	5 lbs
0932	26"	Strapless Gown w/Tiers of Ruffles	5 lbs
0939	26"	Navy Dress w/Lace Trim	5 lbs

Individually packed

Ideal 1959

THE BEAUTIFUL REVLON DOLL

America's most famous fashion model doll . . . with the figure of a teen-ager and the face of an angel. Turning waist enables her to bend forward and backward and twist around in graceful poses. With "magic-touch" skirt and rooted dance hair that can be shampooed and waved. In lavish, high style dress with crinoline, high heeled shoes, sheer nylon hosiery, pearl necklace and earrings.

She's a wonderful doll . . . she's IDEAL

Ideal 1960

The following Sears & Wards catalog pages came from their Christmas Catalogs

Sears 1956

Sears 1957

Sears 1957 continued

Sears 1958

Sears 1959

Sears 1960

Sears 1961

Montgomery Wards 1957

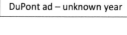

DuPont ad – unknown year

Montgomery Wards 1958

Montgomery Wards 1959

| W T Grant 1957 | Billy & Ruth toy catalog 1956 | Boston Store 1957 |

Aldens 1957
*note the hat box being carried by the pink Cherries a la Mode doll upper left – there is no mention of this accessory in the text nor can I find any evidence that one was produced & sold with this doll
*it's also interesting that in the text the "Miss Glamor" doll is described as an Aldens exclusive

Aldens 1958

HAGNS 1959

Rhode Spencer

World Wide toy catalog 1959

National Stores 1957

Playthings catalog February 1957

Spiegel 1958
The LMR pants outfit above with striped top is one that I have never seen in actuality

Spiegel 1959

Little Miss Revlon booklet –
included in the box with each
doll purchased

Commercial patterns made for Revlon & other fashion dolls of that era

	Advance 8453 10.5" 18"		Mail Order 1463 18"
	Advance 8814 10.5" 15" 18" 20"		Mail Order 4547A Anne Adams 10.5" 18" 20" 22"
	Advance 9212 10.5" 15" 18" 20"		Mail Order 4547B Anne Adams 18" 20" 22"
	Butterick 8353 10.5"		Mail Order 4553 10.5"
	Butterick 8354 18" 20" 23"		Mail Order 4667 18"

	Butterick 9195 10.5" 18" 20"			Mail Order 4826 10.5" 18"

	Mail Order 4944 10.5" 18" 20" 22"		Mail Order 9455 10.5"
	Mail Order 7265 10.5"		McCalls 2162 10.5" 12" 15" 18" 20" 22"
	Mail Order 8798 10.5" 15" 18" 20" 22"		McCalls 2255 10.5" 12" 15" 18" 20" 22"
	Mail Order 9085 10.5" 18" 22"		McCalls 2342 10.5" 12" 15" 18" 20" 22"

	Mail Order 9092 14" 16" 18" 20" 22"		McCalls 2397 10.5" 20"
	Mail Order 9302 10.5" 18"		Simplicity 1808 15" 18" 21" 23"

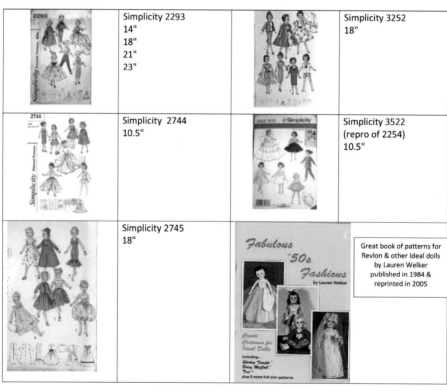

	Simplicity 2293 14" 18" 21" 23"		Simplicity 3252 18"
	Simplicity 2744 10.5"		Simplicity 3522 (repro of 2254) 10.5"
	Simplicity 2745 18"		Great book of patterns for Revlon & other Ideal dolls by Lauren Welker published in 1984 & reprinted in 2005

Bibliography

Revlon Dolls and their Look-Alikes by Kathy Barna
(out of print - available through Ebay & Amazon)

Collector's Guide to Ideal Dolls, editions 1, 2 & 3 by Judith Izen
(to order: http://www.dollsofourchildhood.com/)

http://www.angelfire.com/ultra/revlondoll/index.html by Barb Walker
(Fabulous site with great photos & detailed descriptions of Little Miss Revlon outfits)

Magazines

March-April '93	Dolls	"Beauty Parlor Prima Donnas - American Character Toni & Revlon Dolls" - by Billy Boy
Nov '02	Dolls	"Ideal Miss Revlon Dolls" - by Kerra Davis
Oct '82	Doll Reader	"More Fashionable 50's--Revlon Dolls" (B&W) - by Margaret Groninger
Dec '83/Jan '84	Doll Reader	"Diminutive High Heeled Fashion Dolls" - by Pam & Polly Judd
Nov '85	Doll Reader	"More Diminutive High Heeled Fashion Dolls" - by Pam & Polly Judd
Dec '87-Jan '88	Doll Reader	"So Beautiful Her Name Just Had to be Revlon" - by Glenn Mandeville
Oct '93	Doll Reader	"Ideal's Revlon Dolls" - by Deborah Adam Thompson

June-July '96	Doll Reader	"The 15 inch Revlon dolls" - by Laura Meisner
Feb '97	Doll Reader	"Little Miss Revlon" - by Judith Izen
May '98	Doll Reader	"The Revlon Doll" - by Glenn Mandeville (Glenn & Dick Tahsin's collection) – great photos of 5th Ave's
2000	Dollzine (online mag- azine)	"The History of the American Fashion Doll" - by Glenn Mandeville
May-June '05	Haute Doll	"Glamour Dolls of the 1950's" - by Robert Tonner
Feb '95	Doll World	"Those Glamorous Revlon Dolls" - by Linda Potter

Made in the USA
Lexington, KY
30 July 2018